Porky's Quest
An Adventure in the Rio Grande Bosque

Written and Illustrated by
Lauren Bennett

BOSQUE SCHOOL

scholarship • community • integrity

Dedication

"The good life of any river may depend on the perception of its music; and the preservation of some music to perceive."
Aldo Leopold

This book is dedicated to all the students, educators and citizen scientists who strive to preserve the music of the Rio Grande.

Published by the Bosque Ecosystem Monitoring Program
Printed in the USA

ISBN-13: 978-0615772769
ISBN-10: 0615772765

BEMP @ Bosque School
4000 Learning Rd. NW
Albuquerque. NM 87120

Acknowledgements

I would like to thank Dan Shaw, Wildlife and Conservation teacher, Director of Black Institute for Environmental Studies and Co-Director of BEMP, for conceiving the idea for this book, not only as an aid for teachers and students involved with BEMP, but also to show that there are many ways to educate and advocate for the preservation of nature--through art and storytelling, with humor, and with beauty. Mr. Shaw's untiring and enthusiastic work in wildlife education has touched countless students and challenged them, as he challenged me throughout the creation of this book, to consider how every being in nature affects every other being and, in turn, affects the whole of life.

I thank also the Black Institute for Environmental Studies for passionate conservation efforts, for recognizing the importance of environmental education, and for assisting with the continuation of the BEMP program.

My art teacher, Neecy Twinem, was indispensable in the creation of this book. A busy educator and children's picture book illustrator (*E is for Enchantment*), she made herself available to me throughout the process, helping me in countless ways from offering moral support to walking me through the many troublesome technical aspects of publishing the book.

I would also like to thank Rebecca Belletto, BEMP Operations Manager, for her reading and re-reading, editing and re-editing many drafts, and offering wonderful suggestions in the creation of the book.

And finally, I thank all the rest of the BEMP staff including Kim Fike, Kim Eichorst, Kimi Scheerer and Rowan Converse for their help in reviewing the book, clarifying scientific facts, and brainstorming the storyline. Their work in environmental education is essential to the health and future of our beloved Rio Grande Bosque.

The Bosque Ecosystem Monitoring Program (BEMP)

Since 1997, students and their teachers have been on an adventure along the Rio Grande. Each year thousands of students all along the river head out into the riverside forest, the bosque, to participate in a citizen science effort. In partnership with the University of New Mexico Biology Department (UNM) and Albuquerque's Bosque School, they are eco-trackers recording habitat change. These students are part of the Bosque Ecosystem Monitoring Program (BEMP).

BEMP students collect sophisticated and important scientific data about the Rio Grande and its watershed. They do that using simple tools and following established monitoring procedures. UNM students work with younger students to help them do the work correctly and encourage them to set high academic goals. The data they submit become part of technical reports issued through UNM to inform multi-million dollar decisions about the bosque's management. Federal, tribal, state, regional, and local government officials are all BEMP partners and data users.

The research conducted within BEMP considers how flood, fire, climate, and human changes impact the Rio Grande and its bosque. This is done through a network of several dozen field sites located along the Rio Grande. Students and their teachers become stewards of a section of their own riverside neighborhood and return to it on at least a monthly basis as they come to develop a sense of place and an understanding of the ecological activity in their own community.

To participate in or to find out more about the Bosque Ecosystem Monitoring program go to www.bosqueschool.org/bemp.aspx or call (505) 898-6388.

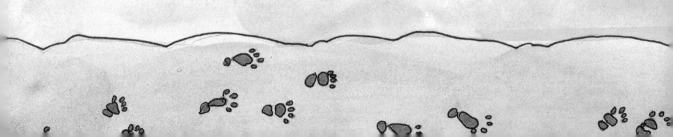

Foreword

The Rio Grande's riverside forest, or bosque, is well known for its cottonwood trees. Under the branches of those trees, tens of thousands of students have explored and lingered as they participate in the Bosque Ecosystem Monitoring Program (BEMP). And on thousands of occasions, students have looked up into the trees overhead and spotted a porcupine. Often students have quietly watched a porcupine hold onto a cottonwood branch and nap while they have carried out scientific monitoring below. In many ways, for BEMP students, the porcupine has become an ambassador for the bosque itself.

In this book, Lauren Bennett, an accomplished artist and fierce advocate for all things wild, remembers back to when she was a young BEMP student. She has written and illustrated a book that imagines the bosque and BEMP students from the perspective of one of those porcupines of the forest. Of course, the talking animals emerge from Lauren's imagination while at the same time the species portrayed, the BEMP work, and ecological information are all scientifically accurate.

Lauren knows that true understanding and connection with wild places – the type that leads to passionately knowing and caring for one's ecological home – is informed by both imagination and science. Lauren has created this book to reflect that truth. It is our hope within BEMP that students of all ages will discover the wonder of their home watershed; come to know its plants, animals, and cycles; and then take action to care for those wild places.

Daniel Shaw
Bosque Ecosystem Monitoring Program
Co-Director

I am a **Mourning Cloak Butterfly**. You can find me in this section too.

Hi! I am a **Darkling Beetle**.

And I am a **Whiptail Lizard**. We are very common in the bosque. See if you can find us in this section of the book.

Section I
Ground Water

In which Porky meets a
Pocket Gopher *and learns*
about the ***water table*** *and*
a mysterious white pipe
sticking out of the ground.

One sunny afternoon, as Porky the **porcupine** and his mother sat on a limb high up in a **cottonwood** tree, they noticed students gathering nearby. Porky often saw students walking through the **bosque**, the riverside forest where he lived. This time he felt particularly curious. He shifted his position in the tree to see what the students were doing.

"What in the world is that?" he asked his mother as he saw a young boy unravel a long spool of tape into a white tube. Porky's mother was too busy munching on tender cottonwood twigs to answer him.

"I guess I will just have to see for myself," Porky mumbled as he slowly made his way down the tree. By the time he reached the base of the tree trunk, the students were leaving. "I missed them!" Porky cried with disappointment. He walked over to the clearing where the children had been and examined the white tube sunk into the ground. Suddenly, a **Pocket Gopher** popped out of the ground.

"Good morning," said Porky. "Would you happen to know what that white tube is for?"

"Why," answered the gopher, "don't you know about **ground water**?"

"There's water in the ground?" asked Porky.

"Of course," answered the gopher. "Those white tubes are wells that measure how far below the surface the **water table** is."

"There's also a table underground?" Porky asked, even more surprised than before.

"No, no, no," the gopher chuckled. "You see, it works like this. Water moves in a connected cycle. It falls from the **atmosphere**, or sky, as rain, snow or sleet. This is known as **precipitation**. Some of this precipitation is absorbed by plants. Some runs along the surface of the ground and ends up in the Rio Grande valley. Most of it, however, **evaporates** back into the atmosphere.

"The rest of the precipitation soaks into the ground and becomes part of our groundwater supply. We call the water that is stored in the ground an **aquifer**. The very top of the aquifer between the tiny spaces of rocks and sand, is the **water table**. The river itself is connected to groundwater through this underground system," explained the gopher.

"But why do those children measure how far into the ground the water table is?" asked Porky. "Because knowing the depth to the water table lets the students know if tree roots can reach the water to drink," answered the gopher.

"Oh," said Porky, "so even if it doesn't rain, plants can get water from the aquifer."

"Do plants die if they cannot reach the water table?" Porky asked. "Sadly, many plants do die. Cottonwood trees for example, can only grow if the water table is at a depth that their roots can reach." "How deep is that?" asked Porky.

"Here along the river, the water table is about as deep as two children stacked on each other's shoulders," explained the gopher.
"Two children deep! And you said that some of the water from the water table connects with the river?" questioned Porky.

"That's right," answered the gopher. "But since I am a land creature myself, you might learn more about the river from my friend the **Rio Grande Silvery Minnow**."

"Thank you for your help!" exclaimed Porky. "I will go find him."

The gopher popped back into the ground and Porky headed over to the river bank.

I am
a **Tarantula Hawk Wasp**, the state insect of New Mexico. I am hiding in this section of the book.

I am a **Downy Woodpecker** and I am also in this section. You can probably hear me in the bosque pecking tree trunks to find insects to eat.

Section II
The Rio Grande

*In which Porky meets a **Rio Grande Silvery Minnow** - an **endangered species** - and learns how man-made structures like **acequias** and **levees** affect wildlife habitats.*

At the water's edge, Porky brought his face as close as he could to the surface and called out, "Is anyone in there?" In the muddy water he did not see the little fish swim up right beneath his nose.

"Hello?" called Porky, louder this time.

"Hey! No need to shout!" protested the fish. "I am right here."

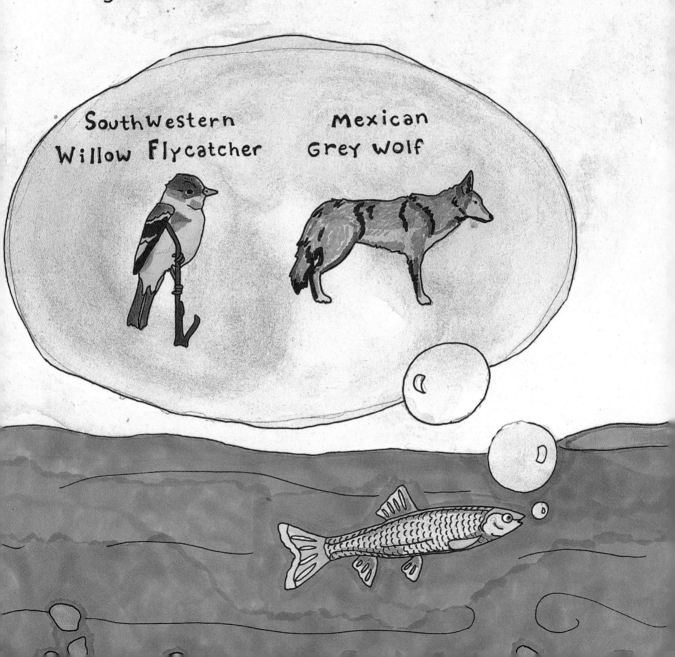

SouthWestern
Willow Flycatcher

Mexican
Grey Wolf

"Oh," said Porky. "Are you a Rio Grande silvery minnow?"

"Yes, I am," answered the fish, "and proud to be one. You see, there are very few of us left."

"In the whole world?" Porky asked.

"Yes," said the fish sadly. "We are an **endangered species** like the **Southwestern Willow Flycatcher** and **Mexican Grey Wolf**."

"But why are there so few of you?"

"Well," answered the fish, "my grandfather who grew up when there were many more silvery minnows in the Rio Grande says that many of our kind died off as the river changed. Over time, the river has become less suitable for us."

"Why?" questioned Porky.

"Well," said the fish, "let's start at the beginning."

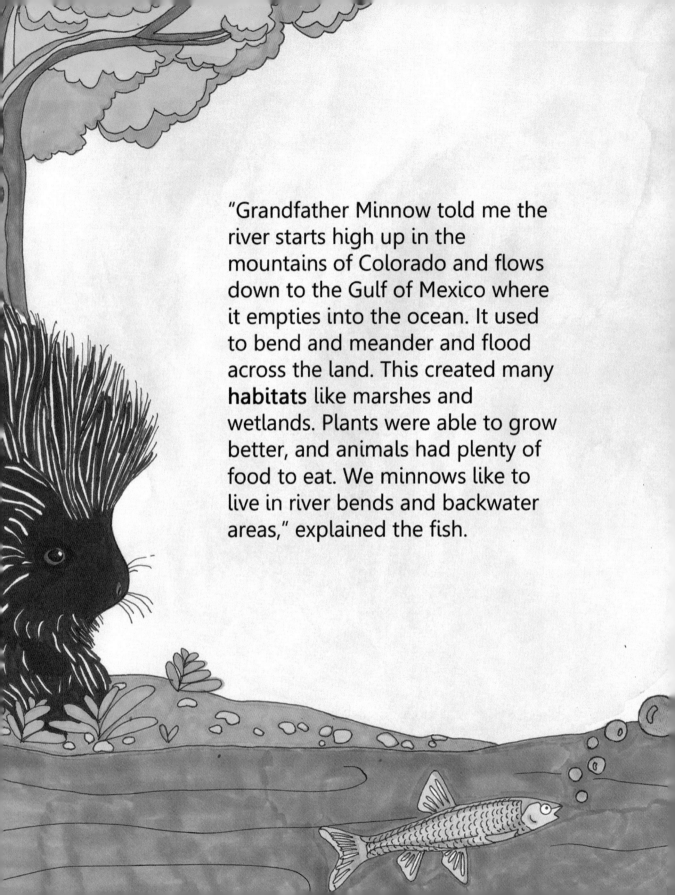

"Grandfather Minnow told me the river starts high up in the mountains of Colorado and flows down to the Gulf of Mexico where it empties into the ocean. It used to bend and meander and flood across the land. This created many **habitats** like marshes and wetlands. Plants were able to grow better, and animals had plenty of food to eat. We minnows like to live in river bends and backwater areas," explained the fish.

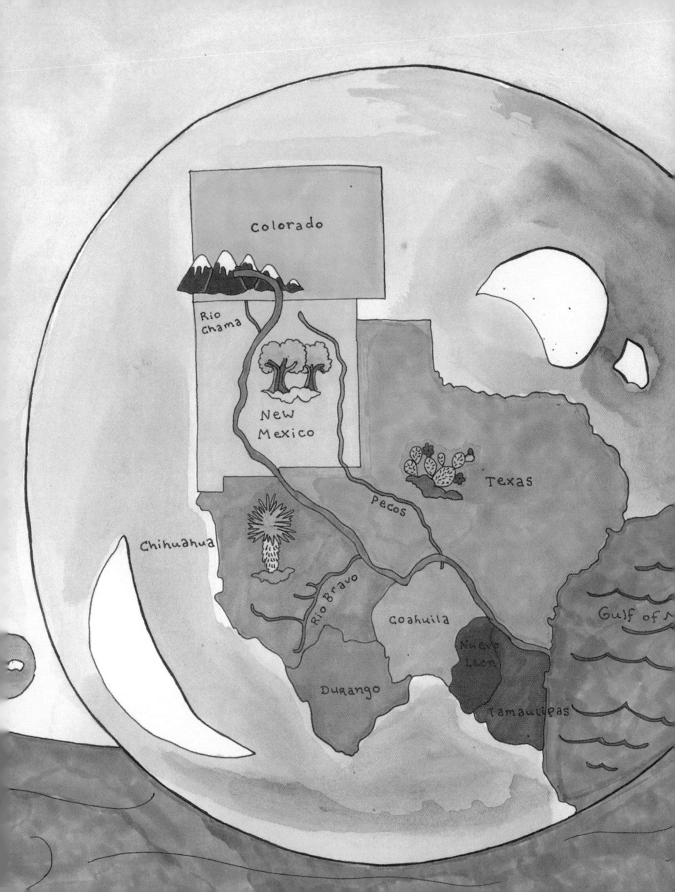

"Now, however, the river is wide and straight. Humans built **acequias**, or canals, to water their food crops and straightened the river with **levees** to control flooding. They also constructed dams to slow down the flow of the river, and today they pump water out of the river to drink. This caused habitats to change or even disappear," said the fish.

"How do these changes affect the Rio Grande silvery minnow?" questioned Porky. "Dams block our movement in the river. There is less water flowing in the river than before. Pollution also harms us. That is why we can only be found in a few areas of the river now."

"But there must be some way that the Rio Grande silvery minnow and other species of the Rio Grande can be saved!" exclaimed Porky.

"Well, there are some things that could help," said the fish. "Even though most of the water in the river comes from snow in the mountains, a lot of precipitation moves into the river from the surrounding land. That is why we must keep the bosque clean. Trash and dog poop can harm animals and humans."

"So if humans use less water by taking shorter showers and replace grassy lawns with desert plants they can help protect river habitat and fish like you?" asked Porky.

"It is a start," said the fish. "Humans need to realize that everything they do in their everyday lives affects the river and the wildlife that rely on it to survive. To have clean water they need to scoop up dog poop and other trash before it washes into the river."

"Well, thank you for telling me all about the river and how to care for it," said Porky.

"My pleasure," replied the fish. "You always have to learn before you can make a difference."

With that, the fish swam off to find a quiet place down the river, and Porky headed back into the bosque. In the distance, Porky heard the students' voices.

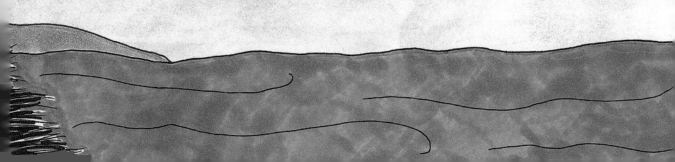

Hello,
I am a **Bumblebee**. I
have an important job. I
pollinate crops that humans
eat. See if you can find
me in this section
of the book.

I am
also in this
section. I am a **Rock
Squirrel**. I prefer to
collect nuts and seeds,
not pollen, but I am also
busy as a bee.

Section III
Rainfall and Climate Change

*In which Porky discovers another
strange looking scientific instrument
in the bosque and meets a **migrating
Summer Tanager** who tells him
about **climate change**.*

He found them gathered around another mysterious object. This time, a wooden post was buried in the ground with what looked like a plastic measuring instrument on top.

As the children started to leave, a bright red bird flew down from an overhead tree and landed next to Porky.

"Hello, beautiful!" called Porky. "I don't think I have ever seen a bird quite like you."

"A talking bush!" cried the bird.

"I'm not a bush," laughed Porky. "Haven't you ever seen a porcupine before?"

"Well, *Señor*, I am not from around here," said the bird. "*Yo soy de Uruguay*, I am from Uruguay in South America, but now it is winter there, so I am **migrating** north to where it is warmer, as I do every spring."

"What species of bird are you, anyway?" asked Porky.

"I am a **Summer Tanager**," replied the bird proudly, puffing his red feathers.

"Say, would you happen to know what those students were doing with that wooden post?" asked Porky.

"It is certainly a **rainfall gauge**," answered the bird. "A rainfall gauge is kept outside to collect and measure precipitation."

"We don't get much rain in New Mexico," said Porky, "so why measure it?"

"*Buena pregunta*, I know from *mi experiencia*, as I travel between two continents, that the weather patterns are changing fast. Many people refer to these changes as **climate change**."

"Does that mean that it used to rain more in New Mexico?" asked Porky.

"Not necessarily," answered the bird. "There were times when there was more rain and times when there were droughts. But overall, there was more rain and snow in the mountains that melted and ran into the river. As we are seeing today, when there is less water in the river and less rainfall, the entire bosque ecosystem changes."

"How?" asked Porky.

"Well, for one thing, in times of drought it is hard for me to find *los insectos*, the insects, that I like to eat," complained the bird. "Nothing is *más delicioso* than a tasty bee or wasp after a long flight."

"Why are there fewer insects?" questioned Porky.

"Drought- related stress can cause plants to get sick or die. Then insects like bees and wasps that feed on the pollen of flowering plants have less to eat," explained the bird. "But it is not only drought that affects the number of plants and insects that thrive near the Rio Grande."

"It isn't?" asked Porky.
"No," answered the bird. "From high up in the sky, I have seen drastic changes to the land. Humans have torn down much of the bosque and have built stores and homes. Areas that were once covered with plants are now asphalt parking lots."

"That's terrible," said Porky sadly.

"*Si*," the bird agreed. "But take heart! There are humans making a difference by planting gardens where insects like **bumblebees** feed on pollen. When there is a diversity and abundance of plants, the ecosystem is healthier. Humans benefit because plants help keep the air clean, and insects pollinate many crops that humans eat."

"But none of this can happen if there is not enough water," Porky pointed out.

"*Es verdad.* It's true. Remember, there are other things humans can do to protect the earth. They can walk, ride their bikes, use public transportation or carpool. They can also use heat and electricity in their homes only when necessary. They can turn off the lights when they leave a room. All this results in less electricity being produced at power plants and less pollution."

"That makes sense," said Porky. "If humans do simple things in their everyday lives to reduce pollution, they can help save places like the bosque."

"*Exacto!*" exclaimed the bird. "Humans must take care of water, the land and sky for themselves and for future generations."

"I see," said Porky. "Both humans and wildlife share everything--resources, habitat and water. All of us should think about the health of other creatures as we go about our daily lives."

"*Claro*," said the bird. "I enjoyed talking to you and I am well rested now, but it is getting late and I must keep flying and try to find some insects to eat. *¡Que le vaya bien!*"

"*Gracias*," said Porky. "Safe travels! See you next year!"

You can probably find me in this section of the book. I am a **Flicker**. Like **Woodpeckers**, I like to live in hollowed out tree trunks.

I would rather live on the forest floor. I am a **Deermouse**. I bet you can find me in this section too.

I am a **Cottonwood Leaf Beetle** and I am much harder to find. I am yellow just like cottonwood leaves that have fallen to the ground.

Section IV
Plants of the bosque
and Litterfall

*In which a **Woodhouse's Toad** explains **invasive** and **native** species and tells Porky how he learned about **litterfall** bins the hard way...*

Porky realized that his mother might be wondering where he was, so he headed back to his cottonwood tree. He was so busy thinking about what he learned that he didn't notice the black tub on the ground directly in front of him. Porky tripped over the tub when a voice behind him yelled, "Ouch!"

"Hello?" called Porky nervously.
"Watch where you're stepping!" exclaimed
the voice. Then a little toad with a white
stripe down his back hopped out from
under a pile of dead leaves.
"Oh dear," said Porky. "Did I step on you?"
"Yes," answered the toad grumpily. "I should
be used to it by now. I like to stay out of the
sun and under the leaves on the ground
where it is cool. But no one ever sees me."
"I really am sorry," said Porky. "Excuse me,
but do you happen to know what this black
thing full of twigs and leaves is for? I am
hungry and this is exactly what I like to eat."

"I wouldn't eat that," the toad warned. "I learned my lesson once when I decided to hide in there. A group of children came to dump everything from the tub in a paper bag. Can you imagine, I almost got carried off in a paper bag!"

"That's strange," said Porky. "Why did they want dead leaves and sticks?"

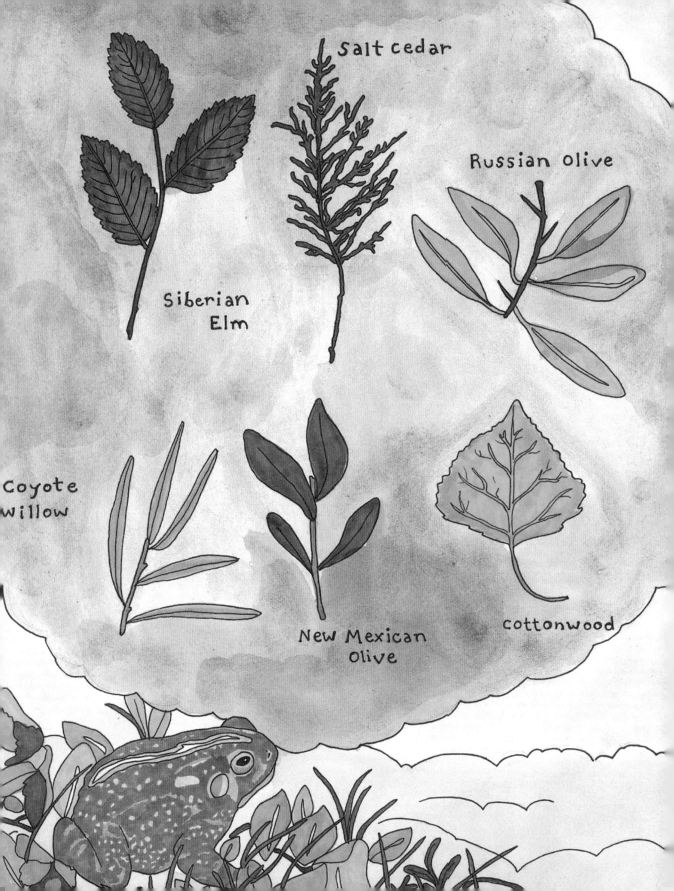

Salt cedar

Russian Olive

Siberian
Elm

Coyote
willow

New Mexican
Olive

cottonwood

"Well," answered the toad, "they call that tub a **litterfall** bin. The children study the type of plant material that falls in the bin to identify the plant species nearby."

"Why do they study plants?" asked Porky.

"Plants help students know the overall health of the bosque," responded the toad. "Certain plants like **Cottonwoods** and willows do not grow well in times of drought. When there are fewer of these leaves in the tub, students know that it is very dry."

"Are there other species of plants that let students know about the bosque?"

"Yes. Many plants that are common in the bosque today were introduced by humans not that long ago," answered the toad.

"Really?" asked Porky.

The toad nodded. "Many common plant species here are non-native **invasive species**, which means that they were brought into the bosque from a different habitat, sometimes across a whole ocean. Some were able to spread quickly."

"Which common plants are invasive species?" asked Porky.

"Common non-native invasives in the bosque are **Saltcedar, Russian Olive,** and **Siberian Elm**," answered the toad.

"But I eat those!" exclaimed Porky.

"I bet porcupines didn't always eat them," said the toad. "Your diet changed because the bosque changed."

"Maybe," said Porky. "But how do invasive species affect the health of the bosque?"

"Well, in general, animals and insects do not eat them. And some invasive plants can sprout in the shade or produce seeds throughout the growing season," answered the toad. "This means they can spread faster than native species."

"Why does that matter?" asked Porky.

"Animals, insects and plants have evolved together over time. For example, **North American Beavers** use tall, thick cottonwood trunks to build their dams."

"**Hawks** and **owls** build their nests high in the limbs of cottonwoods and smaller birds like **nuthatches, chickadees** and **woodpeckers** live in hollowed out holes in cottonwood trunks. The introduced trees don't work well for dam building or for cavity-nesting birds." "Anything else?" asked Porky.

"I don't even like to talk about this, but many invasive trees are low and bushy and easily catch fire," answered the toad seriously. "Fires in the bosque can destroy the entire habitat including people's houses. That is why it is important for humans to never bring anything into the bosque that can start fires like fireworks or cigarettes."

"Can the plants in the bin also show the children which plants are growing back faster after a fire?" asked Porky.

"Yes, litterfall is a good way for students to observe what plants are doing well at any time, even after a fire," said the toad. "They are learning that unless an area has flooded after a fire, invasive species grow back stronger than ever, and that few native species like cottonwoods and willows will return."

"Oh no!" Porky paused, troubled by what the toad said. Then he added "I just realized that I didn't even ask you about yourself! What kind of toad are you?"

"I am a **Woodhouse's Toad**, and as I said earlier, you can usually find me under fallen leaves on the forest floor."

"Do you eat twigs like I do?" asked Porky as he hungrily eyed the litterfall bin.

"I like to eat insects," said the toad, "and other **arthropods**."

"An arthro-what?" questioned Porky.

"I know where you can learn all about them!" exclaimed a **Cottontail Rabbit** who had hopped up nearby.

"Would you mind taking me there?" asked Porky.

"If you can keep up!" shouted the rabbit, leading the way.

"Thank you for your time!" Porky yelled back at the toad. "Watch out for feet!"

How's it going? I am a **Red Tailed Hawk**.

And I am a **Canada Goose**. See if you can spot us flying in this section of the book. We love the breeze in our feathers!

I am sometimes not so lucky. I am a **Fence Lizard** and I have to hide under twigs and leaves or I will get eaten. See if you can find me in this section as well.

Section V
Insects of the bosque

*In which a **Fiery Searcher Ground Beetle**, an **arthropod**, tells Porky how he came to find himself trapped and explains how students **monitor** insects to learn about the health of the bosque.*

And off they went through a grove of **Coyote Willows**. The rabbit hopped much too fast for Porky to keep up, but eventually Porky found her waiting in a clearing.

"Here it is!" said the rabbit cheerfully.

All Porky could see was a little piece of wood on the ground in front of him.

"Move that piece of wood aside," said the rabbit, "and you'll see." With that, the desert cottontail bounded away.

Porky gingerly pushed the wooden square forward and saw a plastic cup buried in the ground. Inside the cup was a large green beetle.

"Hello," said Porky. "What are you doing down there?"
"Well, I'm not in here for the fun of it," answered the beetle angrily. "I didn't know this cup was here. I fell in and I can't get out."

"Oh my. Here, let me help you out," Porky said. "Just watch out for my quills!"

"Thank you!" exclaimed the beetle. "It's good to be back on solid ground."

"Is that cup trash?" questioned Porky.

"No, students bury these cups out in the bosque so they can study the species of arthropods that fall in--like me. Arthropods are insects that have jointed legs, hard shell-like skin called an **exoskeleton**, and segmented bodies," explained the beetle.

"What species of arthropod are you?" asked Porky.

"I am a **Fiery Searcher Ground Beetle**," the beetle replied.

"That's an important sounding name! But why do the children bother studying arthropods?" asked Porky. "I wouldn't know you from any other kind of beetle!"

"Just because we are small does not mean we are insignificant! We arthropods account for over 80% of all living animal species. Observing the types of insects that are present can tell students a lot about the bosque," said the beetle.

"Like...?" asked Porky.

"Well," answered the beetle, "many insects thrive in specific conditions and habitats. For example, we fiery searcher ground beetles prefer to live in moist areas and so do **crickets**. In dry times, you cannot find many of us around but you will still find **pillbugs** under the leaves on the ground.

"Oh," said Porky.

"Sometimes people don't think that insects are important, and sometimes people think only certain insects, like the pollinators, matter. But really every one of us has a job, and together we keep the ecosystem balanced."
"So the bosque is healthier if there are more arthropods?" asked Porky.

"Not necessarily," explained the beetle. "Sometimes it is unhealthy if there are too many of one particular species of insect. There are some insects that can take over when there are tough conditions. For example, if it is dry and native trees like cottonwoods can't get enough water, they become weak. **Cottonwood Leaf Beetles** eat cottonwood leaves and attack branch shoots, stunting the tree's growth."

"I never knew it was so important to observe and **monitor** arthropods in the bosque," said Porky.
"Like I said, we're all important" said the beetle.
"I am sorry to be rude," said Porky, "but I am sure that my mother is worried about me. I'd better go home!"
"Ok," said the beetle, "thank you for getting me out of that cup!"

Porky began the long journey back to his cottonwood tree. As Porky neared his home, he saw his mother frantically searching for him.

"Porky!" she exclaimed. "Where in the bosque have you been?"
"I was exploring and learning!" said Porky. "I'm sorry I worried you."
"Well, never wander off again without telling me," his mother chastised.

"Ok, you want to know what I learned?" Porky asked.
"Of course," responded his mother, "but first let's go
back up into the safety of the cottonwood tree. I saw a
hungry **Coyote** around here earlier."
Porky climbed up the tree as fast as he could.
When they were settled up on a high branch, Porky
told his mother all he had learned from the gopher,
the minnow, the tanager, the toad and the beetle.
Porky's mother said proudly, "Now you probably know
more than any other porcupine about the bosque.
When I was young, I was also curious like you. Once I
went exploring on my own and met two very different
animals, animals I never knew lived in the bosque."
"Who?" asked Porky excitedly.

I don't like the ground or the water. I like to live in the trees! I am a **Nuthatch** and I am the only bird you will see walking down a tree trunk. I am also in this section.

I am a **Garter Snake**. Can you find me in this section of the book? I am the same color as the dry ground so watch out or you could step on me!

We prefer to live in the water. We are all common in the Rio Grande. See if you can identify us.

Section VI
Future of the bosque

*In which Porky returns to his mother and she tells him of her adventure in the bosque when she met a grumpy old **Box Turtle** and a **River Otter** - each with a very different idea about what is to become of the Rio Grande bosque and their homes.*

"Well," answered his mother, "near the river I came to a hollowed-out rotten tree trunk. I was about to walk around it when I heard a voice come from inside. When I called out, a grumpy voice answered."

"Who was it?" asked Porky anxiously.

"It was an ancient **Box Turtle**," said his mother. "He complained about everything--his old age, the heat, but most of all about the children who disrupt him from his sleep as they yell and tromp through the bosque."

"That's not fair!" Porky protested. "The children are doing good things. They are monitoring the bosque so they know if it is healthy or not."

"That is not what the old turtle thought," said his mother. "He told me that all humans do is take and destroy. They pollute the water in the river, use too much of it, litter in the bosque and cause fires."

"But humans can conserve
water and pick up after
themselves and their dogs
like the Rio Grande silvery
minnow said. And if they are
careful with fire like the woodhouse's
toad said, none of that would be true,"
argued Porky.

"Sure," said his mother, "but I understand
the box turtle's point. In his lifetime he had
already seen a lot of difficult changes that were
caused by humans. Every careless thing humans do
adds up, and then that thing is not so little anymore."

"The turtle believed that at some point pollution, climate change and overuse of natural resources would completely destroy the bosque."
"He was an angry turtle wasn't he?" said Porky.

"Yes, he was," chuckled Porky's mother. "But we do not have to believe that what the turtle described is the only future for the river and the bosque. As I was saying, I met another animal, one who looked at everything with a different perspective."

"Which animal was that?" asked Porky.

"After I spoke to the turtle I walked to the river bank to think," explained his mother. "At the water's edge, a **River Otter** swam up."

"An otter!" exclaimed Porky. "Otters don't live around here!"

"Otters used to live all along the Rio Grande," explained his mother. "But sadly, it is believed that the entire population of otters in New Mexico disappeared."

"Why?" wailed Porky.

"Because of river pollution, loss of habitat and trapping," answered his mother.

"If all of the river otters are gone, then how did you see one?" questioned Porky.

"Some humans have relocated river otters into the Rio Grande from other areas," explained Porky's mother. "They know that river otters belong here as an important part of the ecosystem that keep the river balanced and healthy."

"Wasn't the otter sad that he was one of the only otters in the entire Rio Grande?" asked Porky.

"Actually, he was hopeful," answered his mother. "He believed that if humans took action to reduce pollution, fire and climate change, the river and bosque could become healthy again."

"What would a healthy Rio Grande look like?" asked Porky.

"I will tell you what the otter told me," said Porky's mother. "Imagine the river and the bosque as they are now, but with more water--clean water. Imagine an abundance of native plants and fewer non-native invasive species. Imagine healthy tall cottonwoods and a balance of insects. Imagine no trash or dog poop on the ground or in the river. And finally, imagine a **romp** of otters swimming and playing in the river alongside schools of silvery minnow while groups of kids play and learn at the river's edge."

"It's beautiful!" exclaimed Porky. "Can the river really look like that?"

"Yes, it can if humans of every age do their part to take care of the bosque and the river. A child riding her bike to school, conserving water, unplugging electronics or turning off the lights in her house is actually saving the otters and the cottonwoods."

"That is amazing!" said Porky happily. "Is there anything else they can do?"

"Yes," answered Porky's mother, "one very big thing. They need to spend time in the bosque and they need to enjoy it. The more people learn about the bosque, the more they realize how important and beautiful and connected to their own survival it is."

Porky started to agree but yawned before
he could say anything.
"I know this is all a lot to hear," said
    Porky's mother. "Now, it is time for us
    to rest."

"Ok," yawned Porky.
"I can't wait until the
bosque and the river
look the way the
otter described!"
Porky's mother
smiled. "It will," she
said. "I know it will."

Glossary

Acequia - Spanish word for "irrigation canal" used to water crops in New Mexico

Aquifer - Underground layer of rocks and soil that holds water

Arthropod- Animals with jointed legs and exoskeletons like insects or spiders

Atmosphere - The many gasses that are surrounding the earth's surface

Bosque - Spanish for forest; in New Mexico it is used to describe a riverside forest

Climate change - How long-term weather conditions across the planet are different over time (Shaw)

Ecosystem - Both living and non-living parts of an environment that interact with each other to create habitat (Shaw)

Endangered Species - A species of animal whose numbers left on earth are so small that the entire species is likely to become extinct

Evaporate – The action of a liquid or other substance transforming into a gas or vapor

Exotic- An introduced species

Exoskeleton - A hard shell-like covering on some insects, especially arthropods like beetles

Greenhouse Gases – Gases that trap heat in the atmosphere

Ground Water – Water that is contained underground in the tiny spaces between rocks and soil

Habitat – The physical location where a plant or animal lives, consisting of food, water, shelter, and space (Shaw)

Habitat Loss - When a specific habitat is changed in a way that makes it unsuitable for the species that live there

Invasive Species – A species of plant or animal introduced to an area that takes over and becomes a threat to native species

Invertebrates – Animals, like insects and spiders, that don't have backbones (Shaw)

Jetty Jacks – Metal structures used to stabilize a river channel and prevent flooding

Levee – A barrier like a dam built to prevent a river from overflowing

Litterfall – Plant matter that falls off of living plants and collects on the ground

Migration – Moving from one place to another and back again on a regular basis (Shaw)

Monitoring – Studying a particular condition, like weather or pollution, over time (Shaw)

Native species – A species that is present in a habitat without having been introduced by humans

Precipitation – A gas that transforms to moisture and usually falls in the form of rain, snow, sleet or hail

Rainfall Gauge – An instrument placed outside to measure the amount of precipitation that falls over a period of time

Romp – Refers to a group of otters

"Scoop the Poop" – To properly dispose of dog poop in trash cans so that it does not flow into the river and contaminate the water

Species – A grouping of one type of organism

Vertebrates – Animals with backbones including fish, amphibians, reptiles, birds and mammals

Water Table – The distance below the ground where ground water is stored

Made in the USA
Lexington, KY
15 August 2013